ASK THE HEADOC

ASK THE HEADOC

Things People Want to Know

Dr. Ken Headen

Amazon

The characters and events portrayed in this book are fictitious. Any similarity to real persons, living or dead, is coincidental and not intended by the author.

No part of this book may be reproduced, or stored in a retrieval system, or transmitted in any form or by any means, electronic, mechanical, photocopying, recording, or otherwise, without express written permission of the publisher.

Cover design by: Art Painter
Library of Congress Control Number: 2018675309
Printed in the United States of America

ASK THE HEADOC

CONTENTS

FOREWORD

I thought this book might answer some of the questions that the average person might have about psychiatry in general based on my individual experience of life. I'm hoping it will be found to be enjoyable and not boring. Please don't take it too seriously. If you have an interest in a mental health career it may be especially fun to read. It should be both informative and entertaining to read.

As we grow older it becomes more obvious and more real that at some point in the future we must leave this earth. Yet still the world and life in general will continue where we left off. Sometimes I feel bad that I won't see how it all turns out. I find some comfort in knowing that no one else will either. There will just be future generations to repeat the cycle and there is hope they learn from the mistakes we made just as that opportunity was given to us.

When we stare at the stars of the infinite heavens we see ourselves as part of the whole. A belief that nothing is impossible assures me that maybe I won't really die but only pass into another reality of consciousness. I could have a new body and mind if God sees that fitting. This old body and mind fades over time. I am thankful for the time I was given because I've known many whose time was shorter. It happened here on earth and there is no reason it can't happen again at another time and place for both you and I.

I practiced psychiatry for over 25 years which I feel qualifies me to have knowledge enough to be worthy of sharing with those who still read. My life experience has been just one of many but every experience of life is unique even though some are more interesting than others. Anyway, writing this book seemed like a good idea at the time so hopefully it will be worth the time and paper.

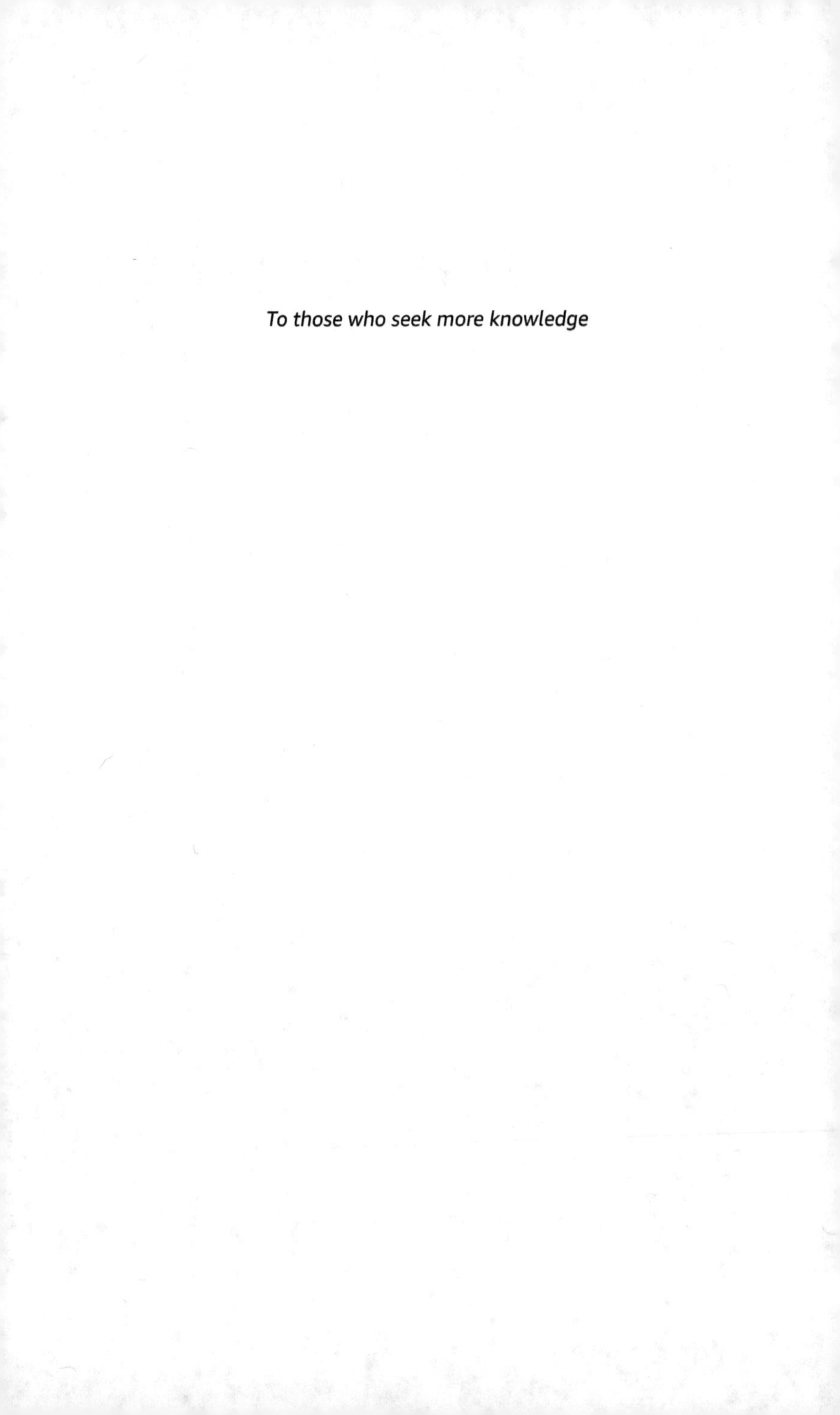

To those who seek more knowledge

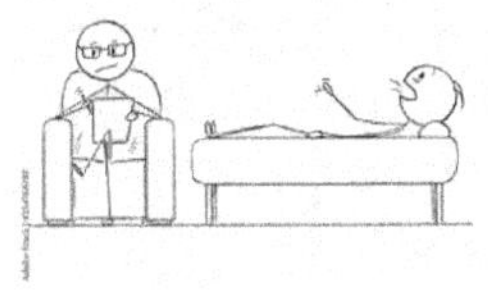

CHAPTER 1

Why Psychiatry?

Just like most people in general I had little understanding of the role of a psychiatrist before medical school. During the third year of med school students serve clerkships on all of the major specialties such as OB/GYN, Surgery, Internal Medicine, and Psychiatry. Most students would likely avoid Psychiatry if avoiding it were a choice but mental health care is equally important as the others. It's just different and involves work with something you can't see with your eyes known as the mind. I believe this was most intriguing to me. Understanding why a person behaves in a certain manner and when an intervention is warranted is always interesting to me.

The word "crazy" is offensive and should never

be used in the context of addressing a person. Yet that is exactly what many people are accustomed to thinking when the topic of mental health is mentioned. No one wishes to be thought of as crazy. The suggestion of getting help when it may be needed will often trigger the response of "I'm not crazy." It's funny how many of the patients I dealt with were often the most sane one in their family but somehow were scapegoated into playing the role of the one who is ill. Usually the people who need help the most are oblivious in denial of having a mental or behavioral issue.

People aren't crazy but the situations people often find themselves in can be quite crazy because they feel as if they have no control. Everyone should learn the Serenity Prayer as a guide to maintain sanity. The prayer asks God to grant the serenity to accept the things that cannot be changed, the courage to change the things that can be changed and the wisdom to know the difference. As I wrote about in "Big Dreams" all we really have control of is choices that we make all of which have consequences.

It would be mind blowing to try and comprehend everything set in motion just for us to exist. The electrons spin around the atoms which make up the molecules making up the cells making up the organs of our bodies. The blood is pumped through our arteries and veins. Within a year practically all the cells in our bodies are totally replaced and we are a different being.

All the while the earth spins on its axis at thousands of miles per hour tilting while circling the sun which spins with the billions of neighboring stars in one galaxy among trillions of other galaxies about this universe. Traveling at a speed of 186,000 miles a second would take many thousands of light years to cross our galaxy. The heavens are too vast for our small minds to comprehend. These dynamics are in motion 24 hours a day non stop to make it possible for you and I to exist yet it appears to us that nothing is happening. I think that is crazy. It illustrates how little control we have over anything.

Psychiatry boils down to helping people make their best choices and feel some sense of being in control of their lives. Even the psychiatrist has limited control over the patient he/she chooses to treat. A patient can choose to take their medicine and keep their appointment or not.

Attempting to be in control creates something we know as anxiety. Anxiety is a result of our fight or flight response which is the main part of our survival instinct. Social Anxiety Disorder is the most common psychiatric disorder in America that affects the highest functioning among us. Symptoms include fear of social situations that is out of proportion to the circumstance. Fear of saying the wrong thing around others, fear of being judged negatively by others, avoiding public situations. This condition is treatable but the vast majority suffering never seek professional treatment.

Sociology is basically a study of behavior of groups of people. In my first book, Evolution of a Psychiatrist, Against the Odds, I wrote rather crudely about the amateur project my friend Lawrence and I took on in college addressing common observations among our peers and the differences in behaviors deviating from the accepted norms. At the time we were immature and just doing it for fun. My current writing style involves more insight and less of documenting just what happened. I have developed the practice of expression without the use of potentially offensive content. Still most of our observations were on point.

Over the past 20 years there has been a shift in what is acceptable behavior in society. There has been cancel culture, wokeness, me too. The world is a much different place today. The internet and social media have exploded information and misinformation. We see news as it happens. Artificial Intelligence will take us to another level. There is more information at our fingertips than we know what to do with. It is now possible to earn the highest degrees without ever leaving the house if a person chooses to be that motivated.

In 2021-22 I instructed a course of Brain and Behavior at Winston-Salem State University to undergraduate psychology majors. I was able to see how much I have grown over the years through observing different levels of motivation of students. Having spent a career in the professional world taught me a disciplined way of thinking that required a certain passion for learning. Except for a few, this seemed to be lacking in 20 year old college students today. I suppose for most students the goal may be an A or B in the class and not a goal of becoming a doctor some day.

So what would it take at such a young age if the goal is becoming a psychiatrist? Even I was clueless at age 20. I know that the competition has become much greater since my time. I'm a pretty smart guy but I learned early that there's a lot more too it than just being smart. Most doctors were groomed from childhood by parents and others to be competitive when the time comes. This grooming instills a certain confidence and understanding that most peers may not possess.

Let's say a young girl or boy has straight A's through high school and they wish to be a doctor one day what would the process be? Choosing a decent college would be the first step but not necessarily the most important step. Who they choose as mentors and role models is probably more important. Studying all the time is also not a necessity but studying more than peers probably gives an edge. Excelling in pre-med courses is highly recommended or it will be hard to be competitive. Those core courses are Biology, Chemistry, and Physics where A's are expected. The exact major is not really that important. Most med schools want a certain amount of diversity in their classes so I recommend majoring in whatever you like. Around your junior year in college there should be a general idea of what medical schools to apply to. Apply to as many as possible so there will be a choice if you aren't picked by them all. It will also boost your ego if you are offered a spot in all the ones you pick.

Gettting into a top medical school or just getting into any medical school is a major accomplishment because there may have been 5 or more students who were turned down for that spot. If you have done a good job in college studies and you work hard you will do well in medical school. The basic sciences will be your greatest challenge before you do your clinical rotations. You must get through Anatomy/ Physiology, Histology, Biochemistry, Immunology, Statistics, Pathology, Mechanisms of Disease and several other basic science courses before you get to wear that white coat as a third year student.

In the clinic as a student you are at the very bottom of the totum pole. Even the nurses will try pulling rank on you if you let them. Being helpful as possible to your assigned intern can make your rotations go well most of the time. Do your reading, know your patients well and write good progress notes are the keys to peace and happiness during your medical clerkships.

I did pretty well with OB/GYN before I was assigned to the state hospital in Raleigh for 6 weeks of Psychiatry. This rotation was less formal in a medical sense and we could rest the white coats and neckties. A tie could lead to you being choked to death by an agitated schizophrenic patient. Ironically, patients often couldn't tell students from residents and attendings so we felt as though we had received an honorary promotion. This was the rotation where I started to consider psychiatry as a future specialty. I found that element of fear intriguing and I liked mental status and neurology exams more than physical exams. Overall I enjoyed my introduction to psychiatry but it was clear all students didn't share this feeling.

Just like in undergraduate school by the fourth year of med school students apply to their top choices of residency training programs. If the program likes you on match day you will receive good news. Most students will match with their top choice of residency training program. Traditionally, about 10% of the average medical school class choose to train in psychiatry. The pros include a more holistic approach to treating your patient instead of treating separate medical or surgical problems. Your own personality plays a deeper role therapeutically. Your mental status examination of a patient is to you what the scalpel is to the surgeon or the stethescope is to the cardiologist.

As a psychiatrist you will know the same principles of medicine as other specialists but you have a special skill of understanding your patients at a deeper level. Not every doctor has the desire for this but one seems to either love the process of have no interest at all in treating psychiatric patients. Most patients in a typical practice are just ordinary people having issues with mood or anxiety. Most psychiatrists aren't interested in working in a state facility housing the most severe cases. The bottom line is that certain personality types choose psychiatry as a career.

CHAPTER 2

I'm Not Crazy Am I?

I have always been a little shy about telling people what I do for a living. People find meeting a psychiatrist intriguing but never seem to look at you the same after they know. Everyone seems to have their own fantasy of a psychiatrist and usually feel they must be careful of what they say because you will try and examine them. Or better yet they may have a relative with peculiar ways who they would like a better understanding of.

Examining random people is usually the furthest thing on my mind since that is too much like work with no pay. I find it more convenient to conceal my profession and try and blend in with the common folk. By common folk I mean people not considered to be mentally ill or with a successfully treated mental condition which is the vast majority of the population.

People in general have common personality traits believed to be due to environmental factors such as unhealthy parenting or rearing. Such character traits are not considered a disorder unless they consistently cause problems in dealing with everyday life. For example most of us may have some character traits of narcissism. Love for oneself is necessary to show genuine love for others. Narcissus was a Greek god who admired the reflection of himself so much that he could not stop himself from staring into deep pools of water since the mirror was yet to be invented. Forgetting he could not swim he one day slipped into the lake and drowned all because he was obsessed with his own image.

Narcissism is believed to be a defense mechanism where the person overcompensates for a damaged or undeveloped ego by having super inflated self worth. Also present is a lack of empathy for others or to have compassion. Narcissists hate feeling rejected and will be easily offended. They take credit that is not deserved. They describe themselves as much more than what reality shows. They may become abusive to overly dependent partners. Narcissists often cannot control their anger and frustration.

I was taught to judge a person by what they cause you to feel. This is known as transference. If such a person causes you to feel uncomfortable or angry every time you're in their presence. If their constant bragging gets on your nerves and sometimes makes you wish you could just punch them in the face you most likely are dealing with a narcissist. You may suggest they get help but they will usually see you as the one needing help since it could not possibly be them.

Most of us may have been caught with our hand in the cookie jar or told a white lie to stay out of trouble once in a while. Most of us will have a guilty conscience and try to abstain the next time. Not the sociopath. Because of lacking a proper guilt mechanism a sociopathic personality doesn't mind lying, stealing or cheating at every opportunity.

Unlike the narcissist the sociopath knows what they are doing is unacceptable but they just don' care. The narcissist feels they are always right and others are wrong. The sociopathic personality makes you wonder why they do what they do but you don't feel that much anger until they cheat, lie or steal from you. These people often are in and out of jail or in trouble for some far fetched scheme. They have select friends due to the many bridges burnt over time. Sociopaths may show some compassion or empathy at times or see a need to fake it.

Borderline personalities are usually more complex than the previously mentioned characters. They can't seem to regulate their emotions. They are more likely to accept help because of frequently being in crisis. The name borderline was given because of them bordering on neurosis and psychotic behaviors especially when a crisis ensues. At worst a borderline person may become suicidal or sometimes violent due to extreme anger. They have few or no close relationships because their behaviors can be challenging to tolerate. Fortunately there is a treatment known as DBT (Dialectic Behavioral Therapy) where the patient has a specialized therapist, a workbook and regular group therapy. DBT is usually effective for most cases.

These 3 personality types are from the dramatic cluster but there are a couple of other clusters that I find to be less interesting. People are not born with personality disorders but develop them over time. This is one reason that parenting is such an important aspect of a person's life. Unfortunately, many social circumstances don't foster healthy environments for child development.

These 3 character disorders barely scratch the surface of psychopathology but were used to illustrate the margin of what we call normal and abnormal. We all are pretty much the same but often conditioning and environmental factors have caused a person to deviate from what we think of as normal. So my curbside opinion is everyone is considered normal until proven otherwise.

CHAPTER 3

Please Don't Lock Me Up

What does it take to be involuntarily commited to a mental hospital? Probably more than you'd think. Many patients aren't honest when assessed because they fear being forced into an institution against their will for an indefinite amount of time. Maybe this was possible 100 years ago but unless the person is considered imminently dangerous to self or others it does not happen today.

Any citizen can petition any other citizen for involuntary commitment through the local magistrate if able to convince him/her that the patient is dangerous to self or others. The police can take that person to the local emergency room where they are examined by a doctor or psychologist who has the power to release them or allow a second doctor or psychologist to examine the patient within 24 hours if he/she finds the petition believable.

If two examiners agree that the patient meets commitment criteria they can be held until they have a hearing before a judge in 48 hours where the evidence is presented with treatment recommendations. Sometimes the judge will order the patient be released. Most of the time the judge will order that the patient comply with treatment recommendations. Appropriateness to comply with treatment as an outpatient is always preferred but if a question of imminent danger to self or others remains the patient must be hospitalized until a safe treatment plan is in place.

Without excellent insurance or lots of money voluntary inpatient admissions rarely happen more than a day or two. Most longer term involuntary commitment patients end up at the state hospital if they have a severe or persistent psychiatric diagnosis.

Being delusional is considered being psychotic but it is not illegal unless the person is suicidal or homicidal. Delusional people walk the streets every day but are usually non-threatening. Most of the people crowding the jails today are mentally ill or addicted to drugs/alcohol or both. Often there is a revolving door policy because patients have difficulty with adherence to treatment when they follow up as outpatients.

So an ordinary individual is unlikely to be locked up unless they break the law. Unfortunately, the jails lack resources to offer the best psychiatric care most of the time. Often the patient is stabilized long enough to get back on the street and repeat the cycle.

Alcohol and marijuana are the most common standby drugs abused by most individuals. Alcohol abuse is often thought of as more benign but people fail to realize that alcohol withdrawal is potentially deadly, not to mention the cumulative health damage over years of abuse. When opioids are mixed with CNS depressing substances severe impairment or death can result. Fentanyl imported into the country has been the most deadly drug in recent years mainly due to its high potency of up to 50 times that of heroin.

Cocaine withdrawal is usually benign mostly consisting of depressed mood and severe craving of the drug. Crack is a drug dealers dream because they keep coming back for more. Crystal Meth is basically long acting extended release crack. The addiction potential for these stimulants is usually overwhelming and some individuals are never able to abstain before death.

I have always considered addiction to be suicide in slow motion. The bullet is fired with the first use but strikes at some future date. Suicide is an unfortunate part of human behavior occuring at a rate of approximately 1,000 cases weekly or more. Suicide can't be accurately predicted but we do know that a person expressing thoughts must be taken seriously. The risk doubles if there is a plan. If there is intent the person must be hospitalized. Unfortunately, most who are successful have concealed their thoughts and plan.

Loved ones never get over a suicide and may be plagued by inappropriate guilt feelings. The greatest risk factor for suicide is not depression or substance abuse. The greatest risk factor is having a family member that has completed suicide. It can be hereditary. Depression and substance abuse do play a role in suicidal behavior but aren't absolutely necessary for acting out. Women attempt suicide more often but men are more successful in completing it. Suicide has risen in adolescents over the past years.

So being involuntarily commited to a hospital or mental institution is basically a last resort to treatment. Any patient answering yes to being suicidal or homicidal will be involuntarily commited unless there is a feasible alternative safety plan.

Chances are you will never be admitted against your will otherwise. There is no need to fear being seen by a psychiatrist.

CHAPTER 4

*Jesus Will Heal Me (I don't
need your medications)*

Now this can often become a controversial discussion with the highly religious consumer. In their favor Jesus was said to have healed a whole bunch of people when he walked the earth 2,000 years ago. With such a patient you really get to test your therapy related skills. "I too believe Jesus can help you out but Jesus tells me this haldol injection will make his job a bit easier. Haven't you gotten better with the last two monthly injections? Haven't the voices become less intense? "

Usually the patient won't have a good come back for that response because just think how powerful the combination of divine powers plus medications should work. You can't fall for the oakie doke when they try to convince you they will take the pills daily because they hate needles when it is only every 1 to 3 months they need the injection. The reason they are hospitalized is exactly because they didn't take the oral medicine as prescribed.

There is an old wise tale (author unknown) about the old man who refused to leave his home when a well predicted hurricane was heading his way. He had impecable faith in the Lord but not the best common sense. He was aware of the times God had seen him through previously. When the evacuators came by to give him a ride on the bus he immediately shrugged them off stating that God would keep him safe. He ignored the urges of the bus driver to get on board. Finally the driver told him "suit yourself but this is predicted to be the worst storm ever."

Soon the rain and winds started and the flood waters began to rise but the old man kept his faith. He was given another opportunity by a boat coming by with a kind but stern gentleman knocking on the door and telling him "come on let's go the waters are rising and you can't survive here." The old man told him "you don't know my God, he always keeps me safe."

The old man stayed put but the waters continued to rise higher and higher. After a while he saw that the winds had died down almost completely but due to the storm surge the water level eventually reached the roof where sat faithfully. He knew that God would never let him down.

Soon he heard the whirling of helicopter blades approaching the house and a soldier lowered a ladder down to the roof but the old man still refused to take the ladder out of anger that God had failed to save him like he knew he would. The helicopter flew off and continued to rescue others needing help.

Well the waters didn't stop rising and eventually the old man sadly drowned. Fortunately, his strong faith secured him a spot in heaven where he finally gets to meet the good Lord. He says "Lord, I prayed and prayed but you didn't save me from the flood. What happened?" The good Lord gave him long stare and smiled. "My son, your faith has allowed you to enter heaven early but I sent my people with a bus, a boat, and finally a helicopter. Why didn't you take one of them."

The moral of the story is that faith without works is useless. God helps those who help themselves. Sometimes we don't know from whence come blessings but we need to trust and accept anything that is of the Lord. So a person's religious beliefs should be respected but as a healer you have to recommend what has been scientifically proven to work for what the ailment is.

CHAPTER 5

Do Some Therapy on Me

Psychiatry has evolved immensely over the past 100 years. I was able to participate in the last 25 years of change. Since the days of Freud it has finally become a myth that psychiatrist allow you to lay on a couch and probe your mind. I suppose we could but we would starve to death. We are trending to the time when social workers do all the therapy and nurse practitioners prescribe all the medications. Suddenly I am finding myself out of a job today. I guess its good it is happening at my retirement age.

It was so much easier when I first entered the field. Psychiatrists are trained differently today with most of the focus on medication knowledge and administrative abilities. The doctors who are locked in to their positions take a big risk when wanting to try something new. The good old days are no more.

I chose to work with underprivileged and needy populations but even that has become competitive. The regulators have seen to it that the smaller agencies have ceased to exist. The corporations have finally found a way to get their paws on those Medicaid dollars which is a totally different population. Merging Medicaid with Private Insurance will probably not work out in the longrun because the Medicaid population holds most of the sickest patients that 90% of psychiatrists don't care to deal with and private insurance will never accept due to high maintenance. The nurse practitioners can make a pretty good living with excellent pay but I think the burn out rate will rise. Everyone is not cut out to deal with the population of patients that I dealt with all those years.

American greed is a reality that people won't confront if they receive their piece of pie. The obvious is that their is plenty of money in the system but the bulk goes to the insurance companies and pharmaceutical companies. The doctors and extenders get just enough to satisfy them with a comfortable lifestyle.

In the 1980's we were told that managed care was

coming and it is here for sure now. My opinion is that we could operate with a surplus and provide excellent care if there were no insurance companies syphoning off most of the funds. Who would that benefit most? The patients maybe.

Pharmaceuticals are too expensive but at least the companies are bringing something to the table. Research and development does have a cost and most of the newer medications have fewer side effects and work quite well. It is a pretty good return when a pill costs pennies to make and is then sold for $30 or $40 a pill. The companies benefit quite well off those medicaid dollars. Even insulin has been marked up hundreds of percent to produce while most Medicare patients paid out of pocket to treat their diabetes. Fortunately, the bill was passed to put a $35 cap on insulin.

The greed helps explain why American healthcare is many times more expensive than other developed countries. Would you rather invest in a popular pharmaceutical company or would you rather just pay into Medicaid and Medicare where the return is zero to negative? You can reap something during your final years of life or you can invest in todays market and reap 25-30% annually eliminating your need for future Medicare. But who has the money to invest in the free market? Not I.

I'm not a socialist or communist but just stating an opinion. Trust me, in my senior years I understand how alluring capitalism can be. We all wish we could be rich but usually someone has to suffer for someone else to be wealthy. It's just simple economics. Anyone getting that piece of pie will never complain.

So is there a real incentive in making everyone well?Actually that would shut the whole machine down. We need mildly ill people for the private sector insurance to work and we need Medicaid with moderately to severely ill people for the need to exist. Medicare is self supporting so it doesn't play into the economy that much. Remember there are lots of people getting slices of that pie.

I think this gives you the general idea of why psychiatrists no longer perform psychotherapy. The dinosaurs who helped train me at UNC no longer exist and a different breed of students enter the field ready to get in on the pie. They don't need to learn a lot of therapy other than principals of cognitive behavioral therapy to be able to incorporate with medication management or to supervise physician extenders. Other than administrative duties that's about all that will be left for the psychiatrist in the upcoming years.

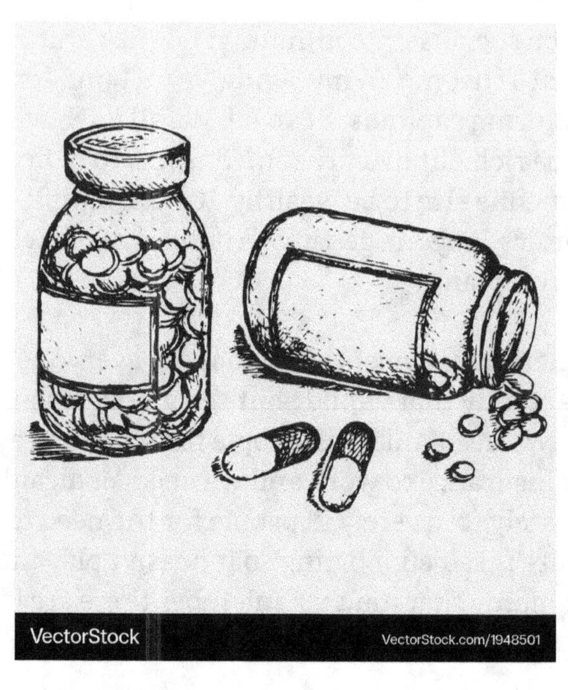

CHAPTER 6

Medications Will Fix It all

Before 1994 Prozac was the newest kid on the block and it was approved to treat Major Depression. It was long acting and most importantly a safe medication that an overdose was usually not fatal. It was the prototype drug that all the others would try and improve upon. Prozac opened the door and led to you not necessarily needing to be a psychiatrist to prescribe it. Even Family Practitioners became comfortable writing it over time.

Zoloft and Paxil soon became available which gave us choices. Soon the lawyers got on board looking for their piece of pie thus the Zoloft defense was invented after a teenager killed a family member and threatened to kill himself. His defense was the Zoloft made him do it. Of course there was a big settlement and over time all antidepressant medication carried a black box warning that "may cause suicidal thinking especially in younger adults and adolescent patients."
Risperdal opened the door for development of atypical antipsychotics which would have many useful benefits in the treatment of schizophrenia, bipolar disorder, and depression over time. No longer would haldol and thorazine be the main players. Rarely, a patient would gain weight or

develop tardive dyskinesia but this was much less an occurrence than with the old drugs. Zyprexa and Seroquel soon came along and except for weight gain were very effective once we learned how to dose them.

Once it was learned the safest way to prescribe the atypicals several others such as Abilify, Fanapt, Latuda... Clozapine is a excellent antipsychotic but caused low white blood cell counts in some patients. It is still used today in the sicker patients but the white blood cells have to be monitored closely.

Lithium remains the gold standard for the treatment of bipolar disorder. Gold standard means nothing has been found yet that works better. There is evidence that Depakote and most of the atypicals work just as well in the appropriate patient. Lithium requires closer blood monitoring than many of the other medications.

Electroconvulsive therapy is stilled used for severe mood disorders and has been found to work in at least 80% of cases. ECT works by causing a well controlled seizure while the patient is under anaesthesia. I think it could be the recommended treatment for practically all severe cases of depresssion or bipolar disorder if there weren't such stigmatized thoughts associated with it. It could be considered safer than medications, believe it or not. Other more common alternatives for treating depression today include ketamine injection which works almost instantly and Transmagnetic Stimulation (TMS). Both must be performed in a doctor's office to be monitored. There have been some successful studies with mushrooms (hallucinogens) for treating Post-traumatic Stress Disorder.

This is the time in history that we understand the chemistry of the brain better than ever. Could it be that there is just too much information available in the midst of an ocean of ignorance and immoral behaviors? Is it reasonable that we can expect to control people from insane acting out such a public mass shootings of innocent people? Such acts have conditioned us to expect another one soon.

The antisocial behaviors mentioned in a previous chapter can be infectious. It is not really a mental illness that can be defined precisely but when we see authority figures such as politicians, supreme court judges, and police officers acting inappropriately what effect does it have on undeveloped minds we should ask ourselves? The human brain is not fully developed until age 26 and for some it never fully matures. Part of the problem with smoking pot is it tends to arrest emotional development at the age the user began using regularly. Marijuana is not a totally benign substance.

I feel comfortable saying that at least 1/3 of the country's population are easily swayed in the wrong directions and will act unpredictably under stressful circumstances. We have witnessed that there are no limits to human behaviors when fueled by enough emotion. Antisocial individual tendencies can potentially explode to have unbelievably potent effects on the social level while society looks the other way. We cannot afford to allow those of us in authority positions to avoid the consequences for behaviors because there is trickle down effect to antisocial behavior.

In conclusion, psychiatrists aren't likely to be doing much psychotherapy in the future. You will likely receive the bulk of services from lower level professionals. With the financial means one could possibly find a doctor doing it the old fashioned way but that is not the wave of the future. So no I won't be able to do much therapy on you if that is your desire.

CHAPTER 7

Substance Abuse

There's nothing more frustrating than attempts at helping someone who works against their own interests. This patient is usually the substance abuser with a character disorder. In the old days there was basically just alcohol withdrawal to deal with. It was a matter of preventing withdrawal seizures and/or delirium tremens. Twelve step programs also were more likely to be effective.

Alcohol is a legal substance but it does a lot of damage when chronically abused. Cirrhosis of the liver is not reversible and usually a terminal condition not to mention all the other damaging effects to the body. During young adulthood the body is capable of withstanding a lot of abuse and neglect. Around mid to late 30's the body becomes less forgiving to the effects of alcohol. The alcoholic mind convinces the user that they can continue drinking at the rate they are accustomed to. Even though there is usually a tolerance to the amounts of alcohol consumed the person actually may drink even more regular to when they were younger. Eventually the body becomes unable to repair itself.

Alcohol and tobacco are both legal substances but the two keep more doctors in business than all the illegal substances combined. Fortunately, the dangers of smoking have made it less popular over the years. Vaping seemed to be a remedy but has been found to have its own set of health risks. There are several benefits to stopping smoking and studies have shown that abstinence for a period of 2 years allows the body to repair itself to that of a non-smoker. Stopping smoking adds years to ones health and longevity.

Marijuana is not as benign as people may think considering it is used long term. It is detrimental to emotional development. Our youth seem to get the wrong message in that it is ok to smoke pot on a daily basis. Young adults should not be encouraged to use marijuana since the risk is far greater than the benefit. Since the brain develops up to age 26 teens using marijuana daily runs the risk of poor emotional development and lost potential. It would be a much better drug for retirees who have lived most of their life but of course I can't recommend that.

Decriminalization of marijuana is still a controversal topic. I don't think users are well educated about the substance they are using. There is no major withdrawal complication from stopping marijuana use and it is considered mostly a habit or psychological addiction. Most problems occur when polysubstance use occurs and other substances are used in conjunction with marijuana. Often marijuana may be the least toxic substance in their drug screen. It shows up for weeks in the urine and blood.

I believe the line is drawn with the use of marijuana because a crossover to harder drugs suggests issues with character because that person voluntarily breaks a law which may also open a door to more antisocial behaviors. Opioids are illegal without a prescription and today doctors rarely write prescriptions except for severe pain cases.

Benzodiazepines have fallen out of favor mainly due to the dangers associated with mixing with opioids which can result in respiratory failure and death. Unfortunately, most opioids are illegally imported from other countries including the deadly fentanyl drug. As noted it is 50 times as potent as heroin and morphine so a couple of pills could be fatal for inexperienced users or even experienced users with other drugs on board.

Many opioid deaths could be prevented by administering Narcan (naloxone) which has become more available. The usual problem is that the person is unconscious and unable to ask for help when they have OD'd. They never make it to a hospital and there may be no one around to administer Narcan. Deaths from fentanyl have recently been reported to be at least 8 daily in America.

Casual use of powdered cocaine is probably overrated since most users are upper middle to high class and it is usually snorted. Freud used cocaine for his depression. Cocaine was also an ingredient of Coca Cola before it became an illegal substance. There is a risk of destruction to the inner nose but less risk of seizures or heart attack. Smoking crack or crystal meth is associated more with lower socio-economic classes. Crack enters the body instantly through the lungs and is super addictive. The high only lasts a few minutes and the user spends most of their time chasing another high. Crystal meth is more toxic than crack but the high can last for hours. Most people are aware of the damage caused to teeth, skin, and the overall health of the user.

Why do people use drugs in the first place? No one knows for sure in all cases but once a person starts the brain can be conditioned for that dopamine hit. At that point they really have lost control but usually don't know or don't care. Relationships become strained and problems with work or school are common.

If a person seeks help in a genuine way early in an addiction they can be helped to put their life back on track. Unfortunately, Most addicts present for help when they have hit rock bottom. Often they must be forced to seek treatment. They have lived in denial for such a long time that most energy goes into breaking down that wall while there is vulnerability.

CHAPTER 8

LGBT+

I don't really want to touch this one but due to it being such a hot and controversial topic there is no way to avoid addressing it. Everyone seems to have an opinion. The world is changing fast and we have no choice but to accept that. There was a time when homosexuality was labeled a mental disorder but there was never sufficient evidence to support that claim.

The topics of the day now are whether adolescents should have sex change and whether a female born a male should be allowed to participate in female sporting events. I was involved with a case where a

12 year old boy believed he was a girl and wanted to have procedures. Because the mother agreed strongly and other doctors were complicit there was not a lot for me to do with the matter. The child did have some emotional issues that were not directly related to the issue of gender. I kept my focus on the non-gender matters.

As far as judgment of people's choices I think it's best to mind your own business. You will probably find most transexual people to be good people who seek the same happiness as heterosexual people. The problem is that they make the majority feel uncomfortable because of it being something we aren't accustomed to seeing everyday. Homophobes may actually question their own sexuality without realizing it and this is manifested as anger or hostility toward the effeminate homosexual, butch lesbian, or transexual.

Personally, I believe it is a persons heart or character that matters and the physical characteristics have no importance. As humans we fear what we don't understand. When we feel fear we may behave irrationally. Many people depend on the Bible to guide them but the stories in the Bible are 2-5 thousand years old and times were different.

Unfortunately, many people lack critical thinking skills. If Jesus walked the earth today I think he would love everybody regardless. The real question is whether we would love him or not. What I see from many claiming to be evangelists is not loving or Christian behavior. If Jesus was really concerned about homosexuals I'm sure someone would have recorded it because I'm sure there have always been homosexuals among us. Yet the new testament fails to mention homosexuality.

As we enter the future it is obvious that sex and gender issues will continue to become more mainstream. The heterosexual community will be required to be more tolerant and accepting. Hard core evangelicals will probably never be accepting of anything beyond heterosexual behaviors. Still the country is composed of many demographics which aren't going away and we must find a way to be more accepting of all our brothers and sisters.

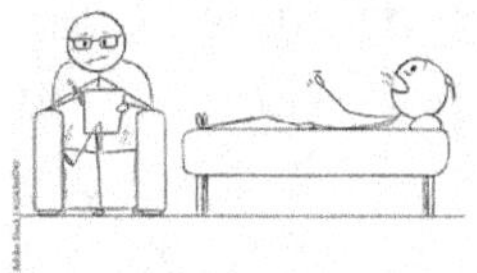

CHAPTER 9

Psychiatrist or Psychologist

The average person doesn't really know the difference between psychiatrist and psychologist. This short chapter should help clarify. Freud was a psychiatrist who functioned largely as a psychologist but the field of psychiatry has evolved profoundly since his day.

A modern day psychiatrist has completed medical school and a residency in psychiatry and often child psychiatry fellowship. Psychiatry is a medical specialty just as is internal medicine, surgery, pediatrics, and OB/GYN. The psychiatrist has experienced all of these disciplines during medical school. The psychiatrist also has some training in neurology.

Psychiatry training traditionally has been psychoanalytically oriented or neuro-biologically oriented. Simply put either therapy oriented or medication oriented. Today the focus has become almost completely pharmaceutically focused. Psychiatrists are paid to diagnose and prescribe psych medications. Insurance does not pay a doctor to do therapy.

A psychologist has a PhD not a medical degree although there is also a Masters level of psychology. Most therapy is done by Licensed Clinical Social Workers today. Family Nurse Practitioners and Physician Assistants have taken over most of the prescribing duties from psychiatrists. Thus the need for psychiatrists has lessened in the face of this trend. This trend has basically eliminated the private practice psychiatrist. The big healthcare organizations are offering attractive salaries for fewer psychiatrists and more to FNP's and PA's.

If you need mental health care today you are likely to be seen by the FNP or PA under the supervision of a psychiatrist. If you need therapy it will almost definitely be administered by a social worker or psychologist. If you are considered well to do you can very likely see a psychiatrist or whomever you choose. As mentioned previously, mental health care has been driven by managed care health insurance companies and pharmaceutical companies.

Psychiatrists no longer have control of their own specialty in the same context as other medical specialties.

So Psychiatrist or Psychologist both don't have the prestige once held and there will likely be fewer students considering these professions in the future. I suspect more physician extenders and social workers will continue to be the trend of the future.

Still there will always be a need for psychiatrists and for any young person who wants to pursue this career I would offer the following advice. Apply to several top colleges and understand you will need excellent grades in Biology, Chemistry, and Physics. Otherwise major in what you desire and enjoy your college years to the fullest. I know a music major who became an anaesthesiologist. Apply to several medical schools and do well on your medical college admisions test. Purchase and study the test guide by your senior year of college. If you follow this advice so far you're almost guaranteed to get into medical school. Work hard to pass your basic sciences courses in medical school. Enjoy your clerkships of the specialties and take some electives totally unrelated to psychiatry residency. During your senior year you will apply and interview with several residency programs which you will rank in order of desire to attend. If you've done well you will likely match with your top choice.

Your intern year will be the most tedious and not so much fun but it gets better each year from here on. You also get paid during residency which is a first. Before you know it you will become a senior resident and eventually an attending physician. You gradually take on more responsibilities but less of the skut or harder work. At this point you are ready to reap benefits from years of hard work. There is no better feeling than this sense of accomplishment. Passing your board exam will be the cherry on top.

As far as what is a psychiatrist and what is a psychologist it will not matter to the average citizen. The system to deliver mental health care is arranged for you to receive care without worry of who is what. You possibly may never meet a psychiatrist or a PhD psychologist during your presentation for services.

CHAPTER 10

*Why Do Fewer African
Americans See Psychiatrists?*

During my years of practice it became obvious that majority of the patients I saw were predominantly white, disproportionate to the population served. Historically, there are legitimate reasons for distrust of the healthcare system by African Americans. Slavery and Jim Crow cannot be overlooked. There was a time when eugenics was popular. Eugenics in principal was created as a means of eliminating reproduction of all undesirable members of society.

This was pretty much the same idea that people like Hitler had. I don't like writing about this but we cannot afford to hide from truth. Unfortunately, blacks have been thought of as the least desirable members of society by a portion of the majority population (White Supremists). Ethically, this belief was strong enough to permeate even the field of medicine.

To start with, blacks were excluded from any form of organized medical care except for the purpose of research. The most well known case was the Tuskeegee syphilis experiment where treatment was witheld from black men as a means of observing the long term effects of the infection. As a result many of the subjects suffered terminal brain and neurological disease. This was profoundly unethical.

During the Jim Crow era the best medical care was unavailable to negroes so they either went without care or tried to find a black doctor which were far and few between. At one time the only medical school accepting black applicants was Meharry in Tennessee and this could only produce enough doctors to serve a very limited portion of the black population.

During President Roosevelt's administration and the New Deal there was still racism but a glimpse of hope for a brighter future seemed possible with the implementation of Social Security and Medicare. Many Blacks could now at least look forward to retirement age but hospitals and schools were still segregated and it would still take years for a significant change.

Blacks, over the years, became conditioned to do without and not complain concerning the very basics of medical care. Progress was slow but in general society became integrated and healthcare became more and more available to most of our society as medicine became increasingly specialized. Psychiatry at one point was considered primary care but this changed during the 1980's and it became considered a specialty with developing subspecialties.

Due to its start with insulin coma therapy, electric shock treatment, and lobotomies there was a history of stigma throughout the general public concerning psychiatry. Around late mid 20th century psychiatry began to become more scientific and inline with traditional medical practice. The public continued to focus more on the types of patients than the actual science though some people began to realize that it wasn't necesary to be qualified insane to actually benefit from what psychiatry has to offer.

Having been left out of medical care in general blacks

weren't about to even think about being treated psychiatrically unless involuntarily committed to a state institution. Involuntary commitment and psychiatry were pretty much one and the same to the common folk. Psychoanalysis was represented on TV and the movies. There seemed to be no place for an average black patient in need of help emotionally outside the church community.

Today we know that people are more comfortable receiving care from a doctor in their own ethnic group. Needless to say there was never a time of surplus African American psychiatrists. I think I was in my late 20's before meeting one in person. I was the only black male entering psychiatry in my medical school graduating class and the only one in my residency training class. So I guess the black patients didn't have a lot to pick from. I suppose the answer to the question of why don't more African-Americans see psychiatrist is there may not be enough psychiatrists they want to see and they are probably conditioned to not trust the establishment. I can say that it is getting better though.

Mental healthcare is broadly available today for practically anyone seeking help today. Even the uninsured can be seen at the county supported agencies. Insured parties have a broad variety of choices of who they would like to see. You can easily find a provider on Google. If the fit isn't good you are free to pick another provider. Don't be afraid to seek help when you need it.

CHAPTER 11

Your Psychiatric Visit

Almost everyone will face times in life where some help will be needed just from ordinary life stressors. We understand better today the effects that trauma can have on ones mental state. Trauma can be caused by sexual/physical abuse, neglect, abandonment issues, loss of loved ones, loss of employment, accidents, etc... Trauma increases the risk of vulnerability to a depressive or anxiety disorder especially if there is family history of mental problems. Genetics plays a major role in vulnerability to stress and how well a person can compensate emotionally.

If that time comes for you when you need to seek help there is no need to fear. The psychiatrist is your friend and is there to help. When you are referred by your primary care doctor to see a psychiatrist what should you expect?

You will have a chief complaint such as " I feel sad all the time" or "I can't stop worrying." You will either have a history of treatment or this will be your first time needing to see a mental health professional. When you arrive at the office you will be greeted by a receptionist who will provide you with a number of forms to complete. This person is skilled in helping you to feel as comfortable as possible. The forms will collect information about your medical and psychiatric history and informed consent, emergency contact and such. A medical assistant will check your vital signs before the doctor sees you. You will be asked to complete short screening questionaires such as the PHQ-9 and GAD-7 which establishes what your specific issues and symptoms might be.

The PHQ-9 is a set of 9 depression questions addressing things like mood, sleep, appetite, suicidal thoughts and the GAD has 7 questions about anxiety such as excessive worrying and other symptoms. These are simple standardized questions designed to help the doctor or FNP in making a diagnosis and deciding on the most appropriate treatment.

Most psychiatrists you will find to be compassionate

during your examination and skilled at helping you to feel comfortable as your concerns are addressed. You will not even be aware that you are being assessed during most of your examination with the doctor as he/she collects useful data directly from you. The doctor makes observations of your general appearance, movement, speech, and general demeanor. The doctor notes your affect and how you describe your mood. Most importantly you are assessed for potential danger of suicidal or homicidal thoughts. You are assessed for any psychotic thoughts or delusions. You are also checked for any obvious cognitive deficits such as disorientation or memory issues. The doctor makes an estimate of your insight of your situation and your general judgment abilities. Much is dependent upon your level of education and IQ.

Most of the exam can be performed in the context of a conversation but initially a more standardized approach is taken to establish a working baseline. Medical related conditions must be ruled out such as thyroid disease, vitamin deficiencies or age related medical conditions. Most of the time your doctor will be able to diagnose you after your first visit but diagnoses can change over time. Follow up is crucial.

But your concern is to feel better as soon as possible not so much with a diagnosis. If you are diagnosed with Major Depressive Disorder initiation of treatment is usually straight forward consisting of an antidepressant medication and Cognitive Behavioral Therapy. For biological reasons it will take about 3 weeks of medication therapy before your depression is starting to improve. You will benefit most by seeing your therapist as often as allowed by your insurance plan.

If you are diagnosed with Generalized Anxiety Disorder or another anxiety diagnosis the treatment is essentially the same. Benzodiazepines are no longer the standard of care for chronic anxiety although they can be used in the appropriate patient long enough for the SSRI medication to take effect. For most patients the risk outweighs the benefit for long term benzodiazepine treatment. The problem is patients like taking them because they give an effect so fast.

Your problem may be a different condition such as ADHD. The screening process is the same with the exception of taking a different questionaire such as the Conner's or Vanderbilt specifically for ADHD. If you meet criteria for an ADHD diagnosis the gold standard treatment is still a stimulant such as methylphenidate or Adderall although there are optional medications thought to be similar in effectiveness.

So the real key here is seeking the help when it is

needed and receiving a proper diagnosis as early as possible and complying with all your doctor's recommendations.

CHAPTER 12

Emotions

We live in the information age and at times our brain struggles to keep up with everything bombarding it. Our emotions are vulnerable to being manipulated in ways that can be good or bad for us. Commercial media has for the most part expanded to master the art of selling to the public. Often we are swayed to purchase what we think we want as opposed to what we need and what is best for us. We don't realize all the thought that the sellers put into making such inticing presentations of their product.

If you happen to be a multi-millionaire you have reached a status where money shouldn't matter but what may have driven you to reach that financial status may still hunger. The next step becomes gaining more wealth and power. The humanitarian move at this point should be to give back and help pull others up. Bill Gates and Warren Buffet are prime examples who elected to donate billions to society. What is more powerful than that! The darker side of humanity may lead some to use that power for selfish reasons. Remember the narcissist.

Experiencing the 2024 election made me think of how true the money and power thing is. I try really hard to always look at both points of view of a story. I try putting myself in the shoes of both sides. This is the logical side of judging situations like the election. When strong emotions enter the equation logic goes out the window. Many factors played into the outcome of the Presidential election. Some of those factors we only speak of behind closed doors. The bottom line is that the Republican candidate spent the money to target a broader range of different demographics.

Race is often the elephant in the room that has always been a serious issue in America. Suppressed anger and fear have festered in white America since the Civil War ended. Still the soul of America has fought a never ending battle for justice and equality. For the past eight years the racists and bigots have been more likely to act out verbally and physically.

January 6 is a prime example. This is not to say that the entire Republican Party fits the mold because the white supremists are just one component that unfortunately appears to be the driving force for a new world order to come.

The Republican Campaign made it comfortable for people to express emotions reflecting hate and contempt for certain minorities. Even though not everyone in the party may feel this way it is doubtful that the others would speak out publicly against it and do find it tolerable.

The primary emotions in higher animals and humans are fear, anger, sadness, and pleasure. All the negative emotions are rooted in fear. Fear also drives hate, greed, and jealousy. Fear is driven by our fight or flight mechanism which is well understood as needed for self preservation. Without the emotion of fear we couldn't act to avoid or overcome dangerous situations. Our fears have become modified since the days of the cave man. He had to avoid being eaten by a mountain lion where we have to worry about losing a job to a migrant. It worked well for the cave man but is overkill for the stressors we face today.

So we find targets to release the manifestations of fear on. Who do we blame for our unhappy situations? It's the black or brown man's fault. Even the black man targets himself out of fear of the consequences for targeting his oppressor. The internalized rage results in high blood pressure, substance abuse, murder and sometimes suicide. Still, all this is based on fear and often fear of the unknown because society teaches that fear is equivalent to weakness. In reality the coward and the hero experience the same fear but the hero chooses fight instead of flight as the coward chooses.

There is a fear among some white Americans that they will be replaced by migrants or blacks. Statistics do show a decrease in the birth rate of white babies. Fight or flight has been activated and it is no longer a secret where. Whether we choose to pay attention or not when fight or flight kicks in it usually cancels guilt or remorse. The person's mind tells them to fight for the goal by any means necessary. They believe at a gut level that their very survival depends on it.

In our case the President is just a celebrity figure head who lacks the judgment to carry out a sound and reasonable plan on his own. He was just used to shift power back to the underlying forces that are really calling shots. The President's main job was to just get elected again by any means necessary.

There were a number of dog whistles and codes used among the population that triggered their flight or fight responses. The media made sure the former

President maintained his celebrity by providing millions and millions of dollars worth of free publicity almost daily. The MAGA movement was fueled by fight or flight while the left was focused on dotting I's and crossing T's probably not aware of being in a war zone. On election evening we had no idea what had hit us.

I had no intention of writing this chapter due to it's sensitive and complex nature. At this time no one knows what the future has in store for us. My wish is that the division and animosity will one day be resolved. This is only possible if our emotional selves catch up with a reasonable intellect. The real enemy is ignorance which simply means being unaware of what is true. I've heard that stupidity cannot be fixed whereas ignorance at least has a chance of being corrected.

AFTERWORD

Thanks for your support by purchasing my book. Hopefully you found it to be of some benefit. Please tell others and you may leave your review at Amazon. God bless you.

BOOKS BY THIS AUTHOR

Evolution Of A Psychiatrist, Against The Odds

Transitioned, In A Better Place Now

Dopamine Hit, Got To Have It!

Evolution Of A Psychiatrist, Big Dreams

Let's Go Fishing, Beginners Guide To A Lifetime Of Fun

Ask The Headoc, Things People Want To Know

Quest For Sanity, Thoughts From The Headoc

BRAIN TEASERS

Guess What Is
Written In This Picture?

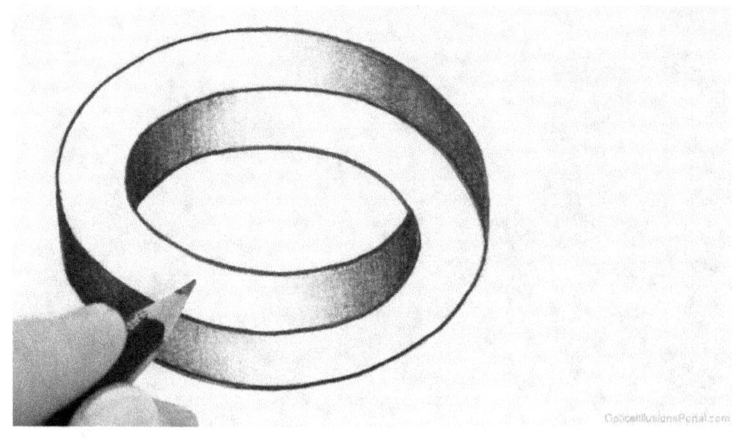

OpticalIllusionsPortal.com

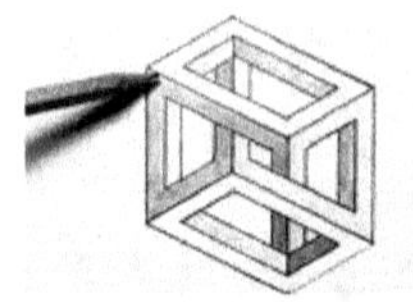

Profile?

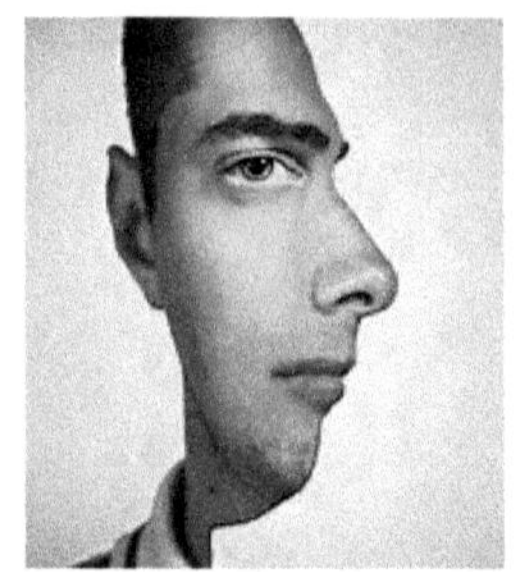

Do you see the old lady?

Can you see the sleeping woman?

VISION TEST
Only 1% of the population is able to find the
animal in the image in less than 2 minutes.
SHARE if you're one of the few who
can!

Can you find the
the **mistake**?
1 2 4 5 6 7 8 9

How Many Legs?

How many legs does this elephant have?

HOW MANY NUMBERS DO YOU SEE?

What do you see?

Lion or Monkey?

Duck or Rabbit?

www.ingramcontent.com/pod-product-compliance
Lightning Source LLC
Chambersburg PA
CBHW061100250726
48653CB00001B/482